SUPER EASY SONGBOOK

CHART HITS

ISBN 978-1-70515-199-0

HAL•LEONARD®

Visit Hal Leonard Online at
www.halleonard.com

Contact us:
Hal Leonard
7777 West Bluemound Road
Milwaukee, WI 53213
Email: info@halleonard.com

In Europe, contact:
Hal Leonard Europe Limited
42 Wigmore Street
Marylebone, London, W1U 2RN
Email: info@halleonardeurope.com

In Australia, contact:
Hal Leonard Australia Pty. Ltd.
4 Lentara Court
Cheltenham, Victoria, 3192 Australia
Email: info@halleonard.com.au

Welcome to the *Super Easy Songbook* series!

This unique collection will help you play your favorite songs quickly and easily. Here's how it works:

- Play the simplified melody with your right hand. Letter names appear inside each note to assist you.

- There are no key signatures to worry about! If a sharp ♯ or flat ♭ is needed, it is shown beside the note each time.

- There are no page turns, so your hands never have to leave the keyboard.

- If two notes are connected by a tie ⌣, hold the first note for the combined number of beats. (The second note does not show a letter name since it is not re-struck.)

- Add basic chords with your left hand using the provided keyboard diagrams. Chord voicings have been carefully chosen to minimize hand movement.

- The left-hand rhythm is up to you, and chord notes can be played together or separately. Be creative!

- If the chords sound muddy, move your left hand an octave* higher. If this gets in the way of playing the melody, move your right hand an octave higher as well.

  An octave spans eight notes. If your starting note is C, the next C to the right is an octave higher.

--- ALSO AVAILABLE ---

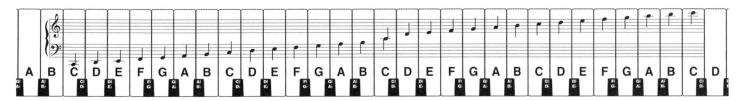

Hal Leonard Student Keyboard Guide HL00296039

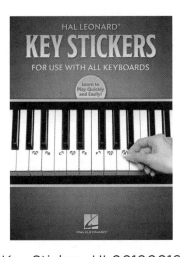

Key Stickers HL00100016

Adore You

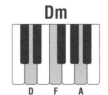
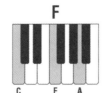
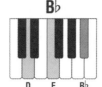
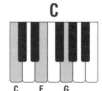

Words and Music by Harry Styles,
Thomas Hull, Tyler Johnson
and Amy Allen

Moderate Pop Rock

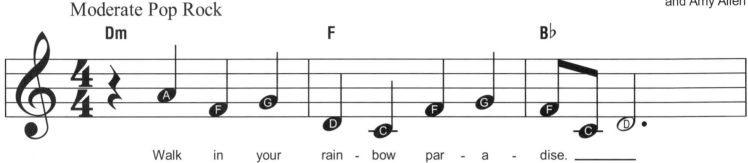

Walk in your rain-bow par-a-dise. _____

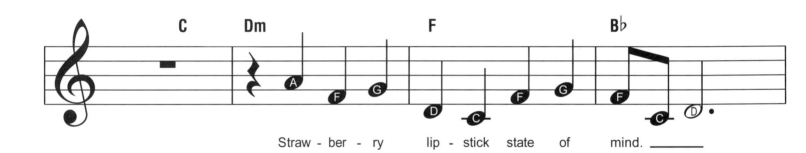

Straw-ber-ry lip-stick state of mind. _____

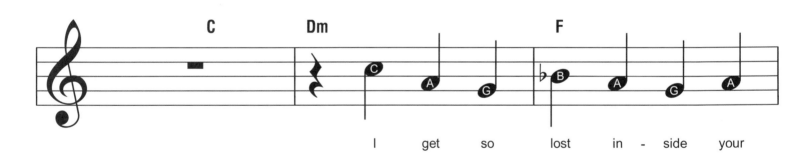

I get so lost in-side your

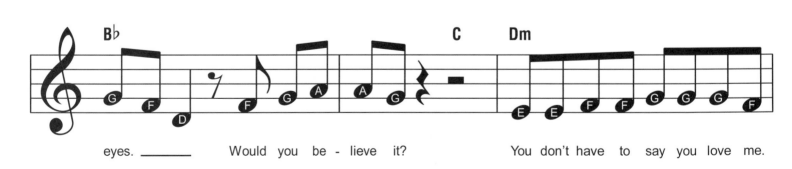

eyes. _____ Would you be-lieve it? You don't have to say you love me.

5

Anyone

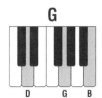
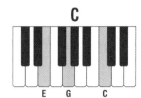
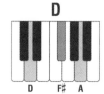

Words and Music by Justin Bieber, Jon Bellion,
Jordan Johnson, Alexander Izquierdo,
Andrew Watt, Raul Cubina,
Stefan Johnson and Michael Pollack

Moderately

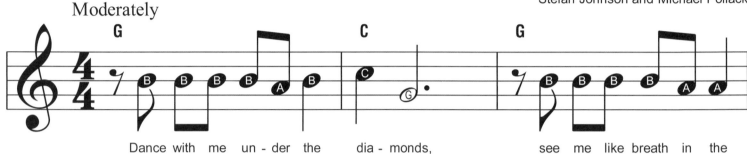

Dance with me un-der the dia-monds, see me like breath in the

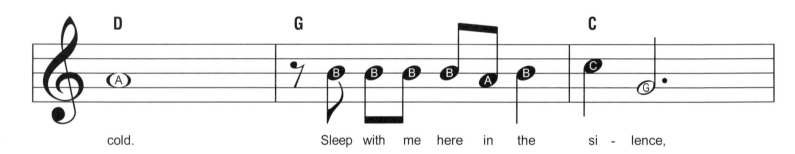

cold. Sleep with me here in the si-lence,

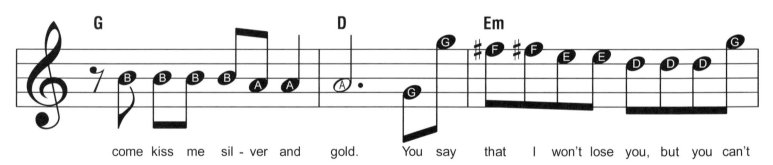

come kiss me sil-ver and gold. You say that I won't lose you, but you can't

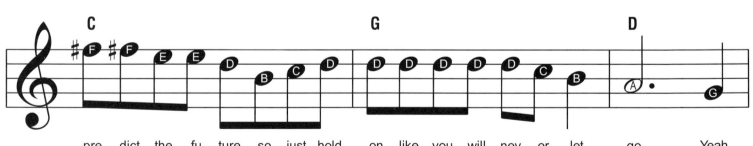

pre-dict the fu-ture, so just hold on like you will nev-er let go. Yeah,

Bad Guy

 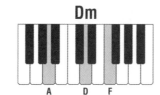 

Words and Music by Billie Eilish O'Connell
and Finneas O'Connell

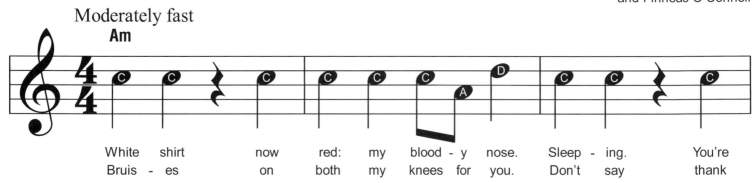

White shirt now red: my blood-y nose. Sleep - ing. You're
Bruis - es now on both my knees for you. Don't say thank

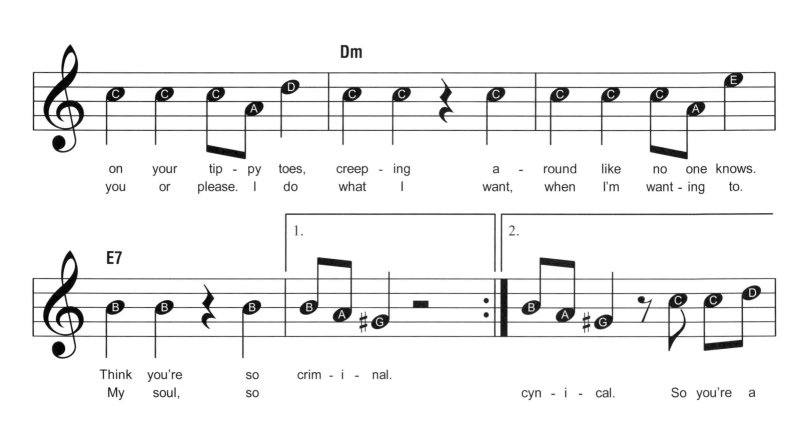

on your tip-py toes, creep - ing a - round like no one knows.
you or please. I do what I want, when I'm want - ing to.

1.
Think you're so crim - i - nal.

2.
My soul, so cyn - i - cal. So you're a

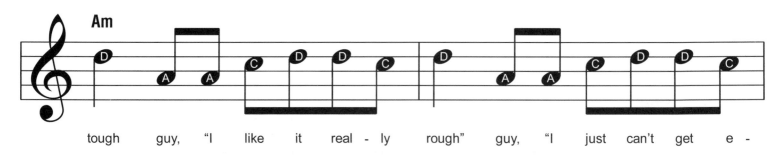

tough guy, "I like it real - ly rough" guy, "I just can't get e -

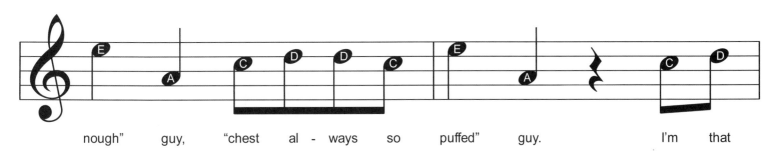

nough" guy, "chest al - ways so puffed" guy. I'm that

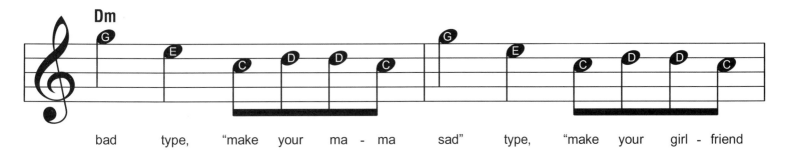

bad type, "make your ma - ma sad" type, "make your girl - friend

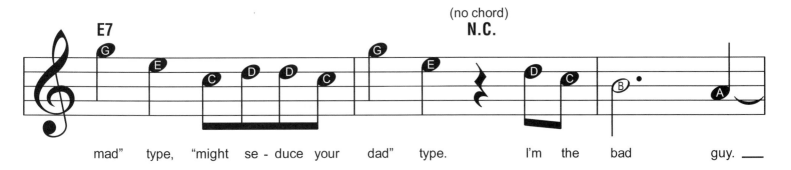

mad" type, "might se - duce your dad" type. I'm the bad guy. ___

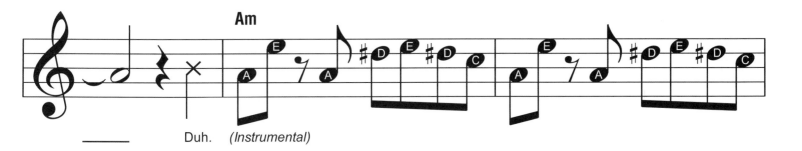

___ Duh. *(Instrumental)*

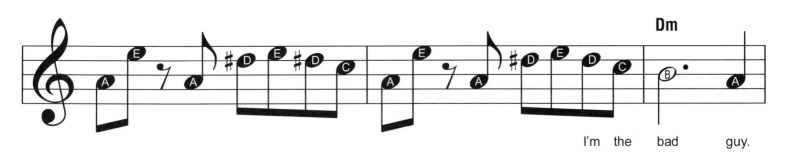

I'm the bad guy.

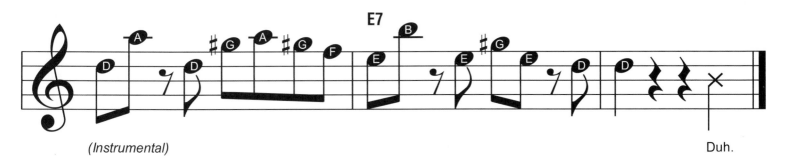

(Instrumental) Duh.

Bad Habits

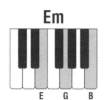
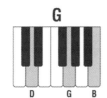
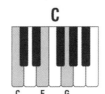
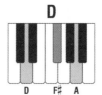
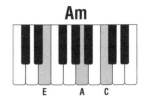

Words and Music by Ed Sheeran,
Johnny McDaid and Fred Gibson

Upbeat Pop

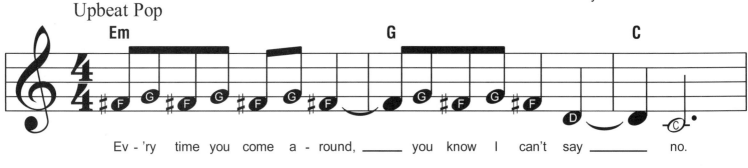

Ev - 'ry time you come a - round, _____ you know I can't say _____ no.

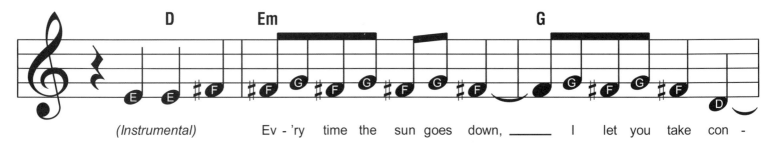

(Instrumental) Ev - 'ry time the sun goes down, _____ I let you take con -

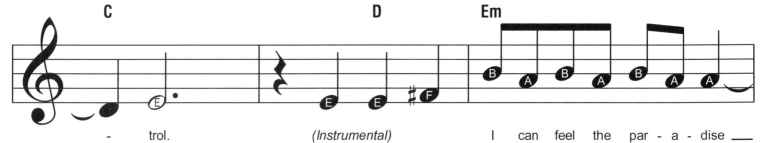

- trol. *(Instrumental)* I can feel the par - a - dise _____

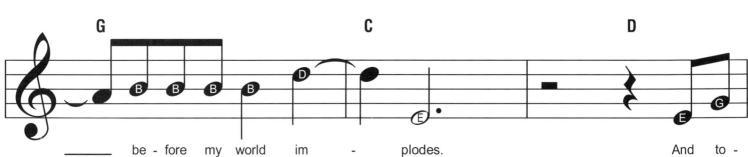

_____ be - fore my world im - plodes. And to -

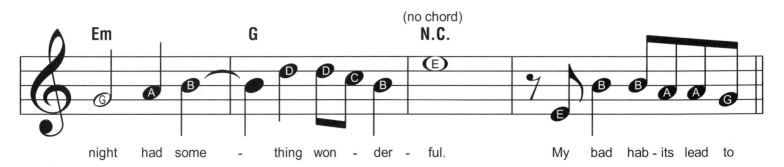

night had some - thing won - der - ful. My bad hab - its lead to

11

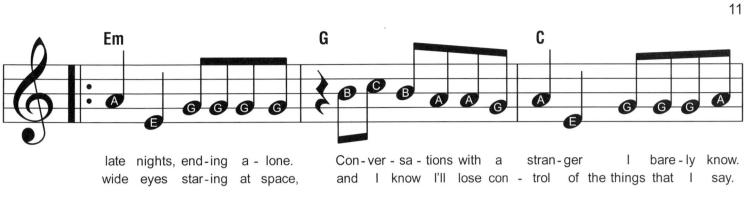

late nights, end-ing a - lone. Con-ver-sa-tions with a stran-ger I bare-ly know.
wide eyes star-ing at space, and I know I'll lose con-trol of the things that I say.

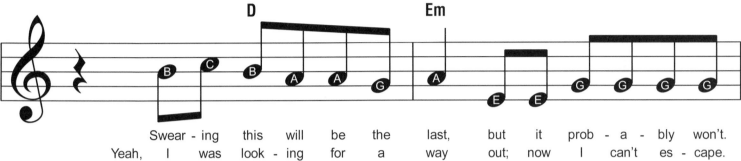

Swear-ing this will be the last, but it prob-a-bly won't.
Yeah, I was look-ing for a way out; now I can't es-cape.

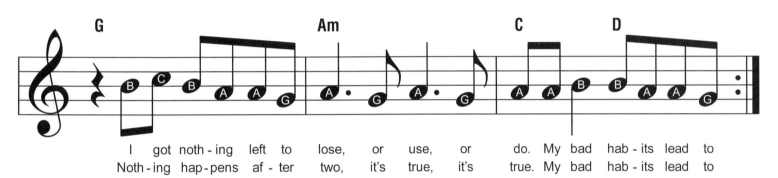

I got noth-ing left to lose, or use, or do. My bad hab-its lead to
Noth-ing hap-pens af-ter two, it's true, it's true. My bad hab-its lead to

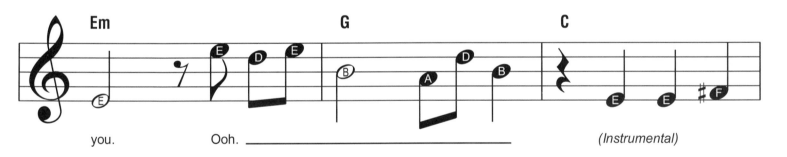

you. Ooh. _____ (Instrumental)

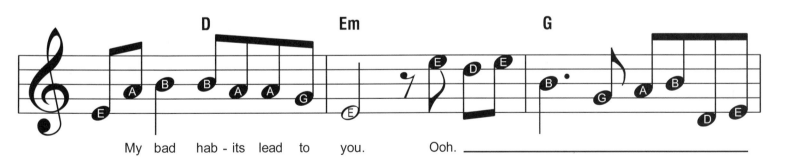

My bad hab-its lead to you. Ooh. _____

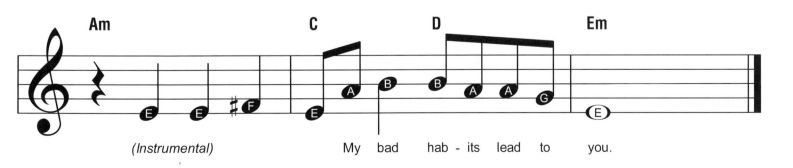

(Instrumental) My bad hab-its lead to you.

Bang!

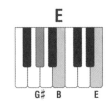
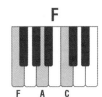
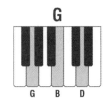
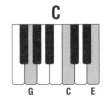

Words and Music by Adam Metzger,
Jack Metzger and Ryan Metzger

Half-time Shuffle

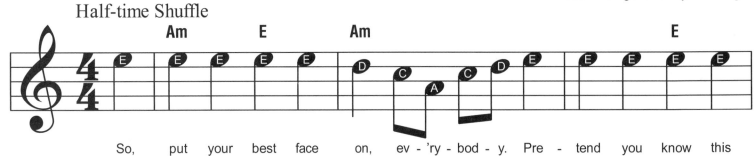

So, put your best face on, ev - 'ry - bod - y. Pre - tend you know this

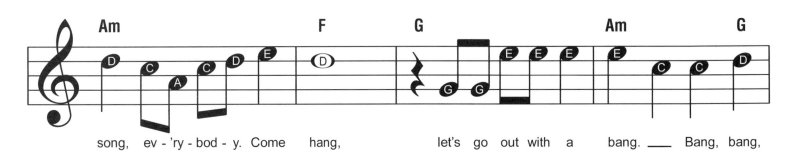

song, ev - 'ry - bod - y. Come hang, let's go out with a bang. ___ Bang, bang,

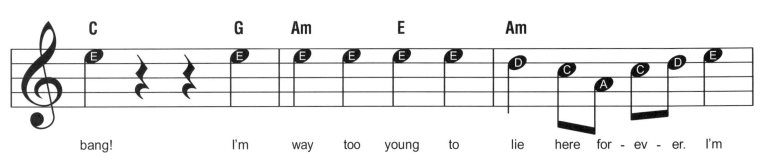

bang! I'm way too young to lie here for - ev - er. I'm

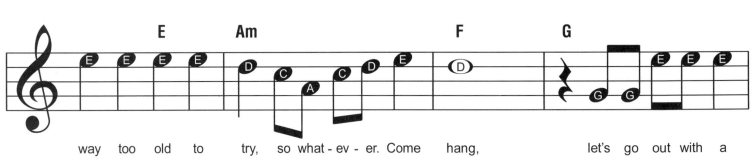

way too old to try, so what - ev - er. Come hang, let's go out with a

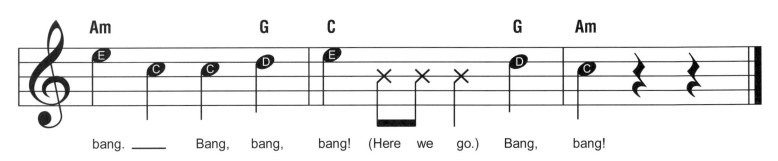

bang. ___ Bang, bang, bang! (Here we go.) Bang, bang!

Drivers License

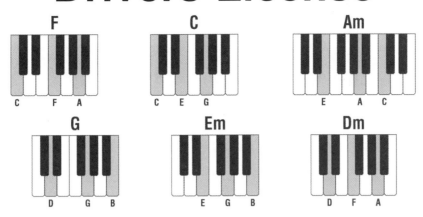

Words and Music by Olivia Rodrigo
and Daniel Nigro

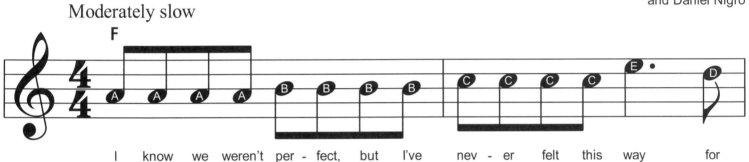

I know we weren't per - fect, but I've nev - er felt this way for

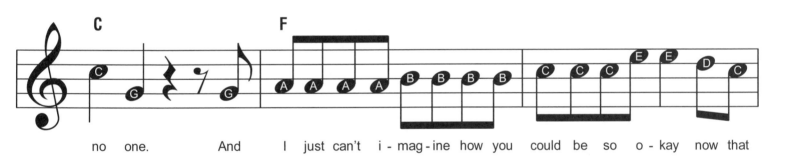

no one. And I just can't i - mag - ine how you could be so o - kay now that

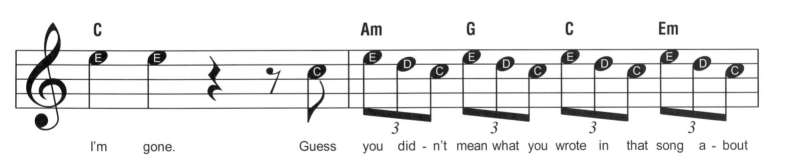

I'm gone. Guess you did - n't mean what you wrote in that song a - bout

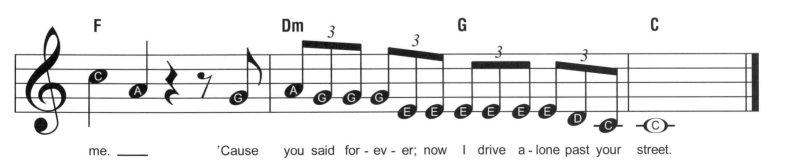

me. _____ 'Cause you said for - ev - er; now I drive a - lone past your street.

Blinding Lights

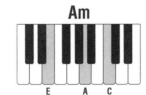
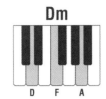
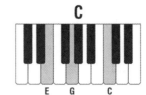
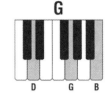

Words and Music by Abel Tesfaye,
Max Martin, Jason Quenneville,
Oscar Holter and Ahmad Balshe

Fast Dance beat

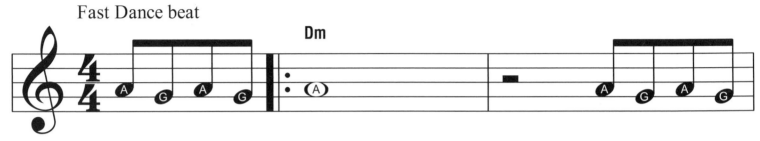

I've been try - na call.
drawals.

I've been on my
You don't e - ven

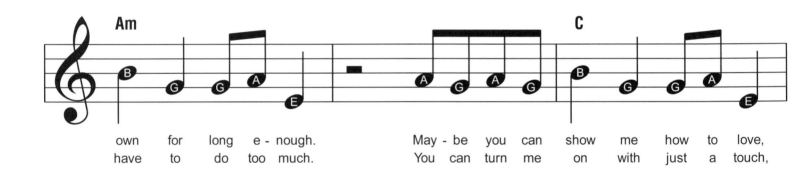

own for long e - nough.
have to do too much.

May - be you can show me how to love,
You can turn me on with just a touch,

may - be. _____
ba - by. _____

I'm go - in' through with -
I look a - round, but

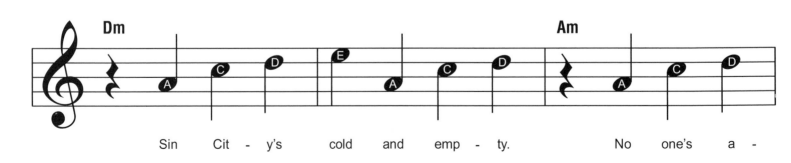

Sin Cit - y's cold and emp - ty.
No one's a -

Circles

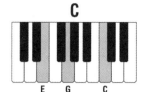
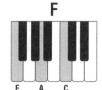
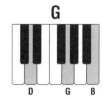
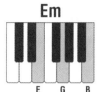
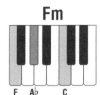

Words and Music by Austin Post,
Kaan Gunesberk, Louis Bell,
William Walsh and Adam Feeney

Dance Monkey

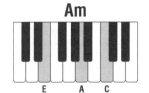
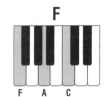
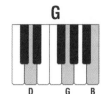
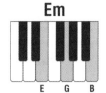

Words and Music by
Toni Watson

They say: Oh my God, I see the way you shine. Take your hand, my dear, and place them both in mine. You know, you stopped me dead while I was pass - ing by. And now I beg to see you dance just one more time. Ooh, I see you, see you, see you ev - 'ry time, _____ and, oh my,

Don't Start Now

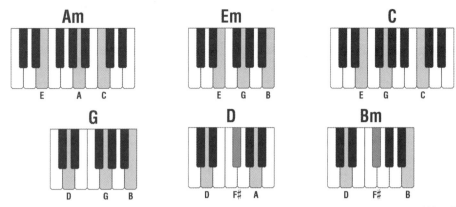

Words and Music by Dua Lipa,
Caroline Ailin, Ian Kirkpatrick
and Emily Schwartz

With energy
(no chord)

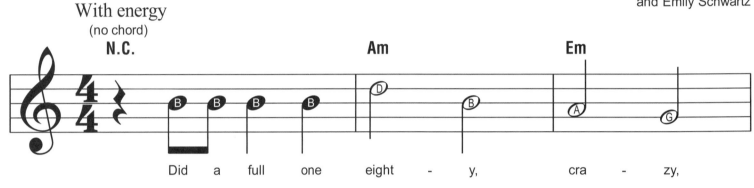

Did a full one eight - y, cra - zy,

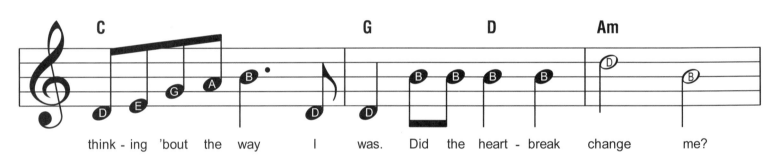

think - ing 'bout the way I was. Did the heart - break change me?

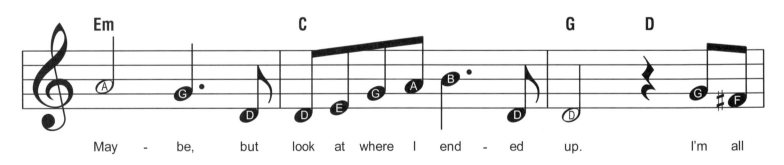

May - be, but look at where I end - ed up. I'm all

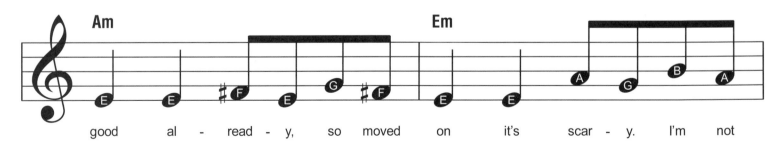

good al - read - y, so moved on it's scar - y. I'm not

Dynamite

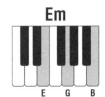
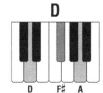
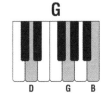

Words and Music by Jessica Agombar
and David Stewart

Moderately fast

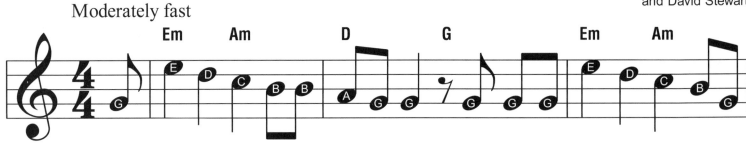

'Cause I, I, I'm in the stars to-night, so watch me bring the fire, set the

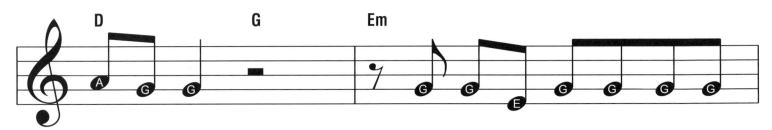

night a - light. Show's on, I get up in the morn, cup of

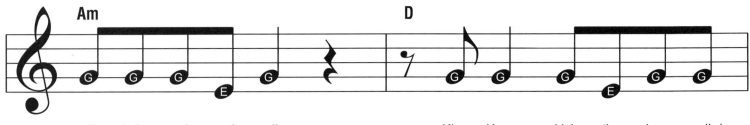

milk, let's rock and roll. King Kong, kick the drum, roll-ing

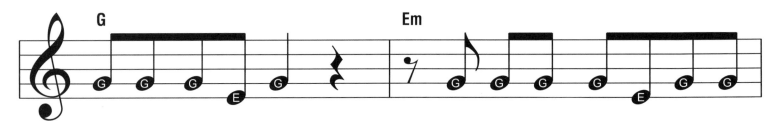

on like a Roll - ing Stone. Sing song when I'm walk-ing home, jump

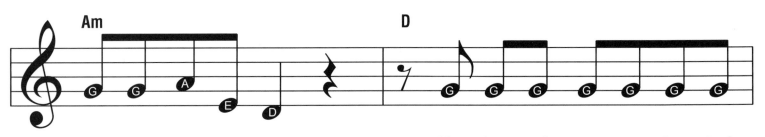

up to the top, Le - Bron. Ding - dong, call me on my phone, iced

tea   and a game of Ping - Pong.   This   is   get - ting heav - y;   can you hear the

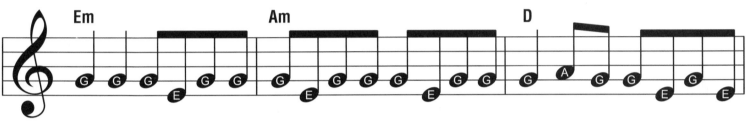

bass boom? I'm read - y.   Life   is   sweet as hon - ey, yeah, this   beat, cha-ching like mon - ey.

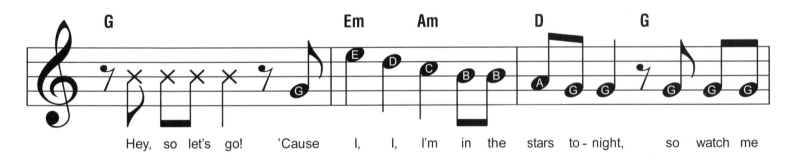

Dis - co   o - ver-load, I'm   in - to that, I'm good to go. I'm   dia - mond; you know I glow up.

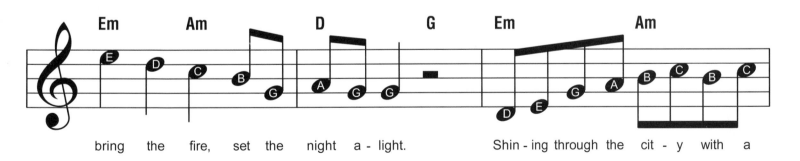

Hey, so let's go! 'Cause   I,   I,   I'm in the stars to - night,   so   watch me

bring   the   fire, set the night a - light.   Shin - ing through the cit - y with a

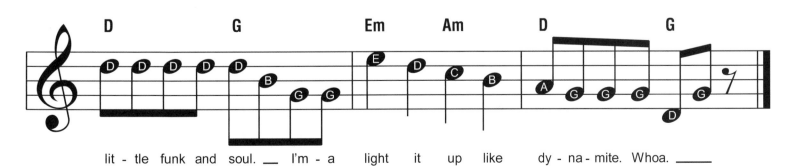

lit - tle funk and soul. __ I'm - a   light it   up like   dy - na - mite. Whoa. _____

Good 4 U

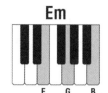
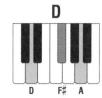
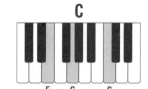
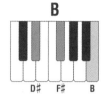

Words and Music by Olivia Rodrigo,
Daniel Nigro, Hayley Williams
and Josh Farro

Driving Pop Rock

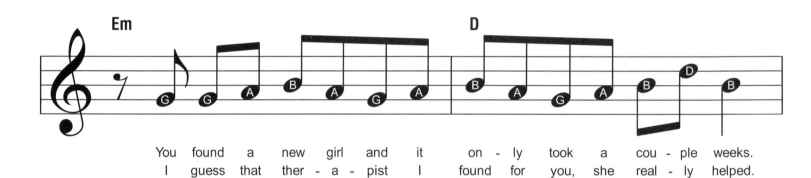

Well, good for you, I guess you moved on real - ly eas - i - ly.
And good for you, I guess that you've been work - ing on your - self.

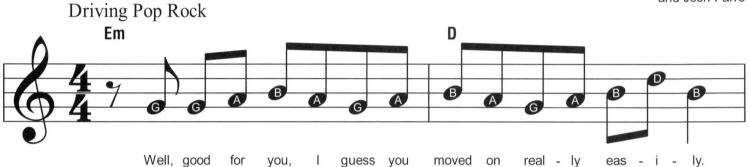

You found a new girl and it on - ly took a cou - ple weeks.
I guess that ther - a - pist I found for you, she real - ly helped.

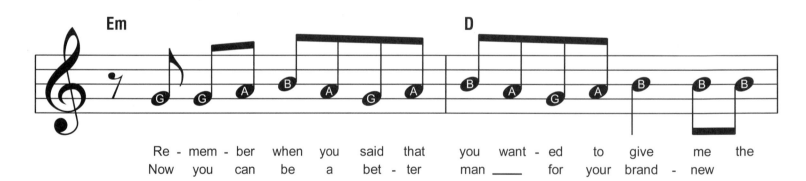

Re - mem - ber when you said that you want - ed to give me the
Now you can be a bet - ter man ___ for your brand - new

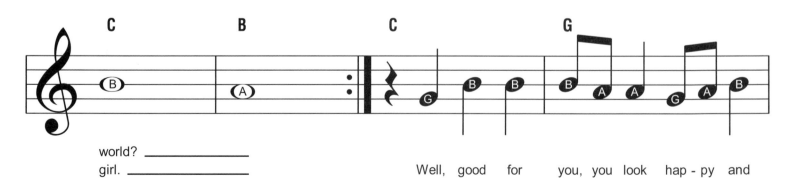

world? _____
girl. _____

Well, good for you, you look hap - py and

Happier Than Ever

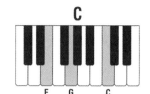
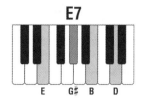
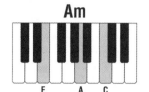
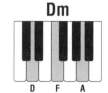
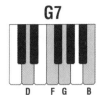

Words and Music by Billie Eilish O'Connell
and Finneas O'Connell

Relaxed Shuffle

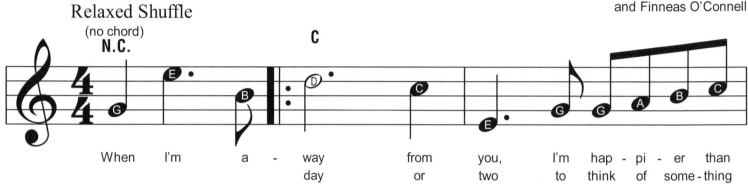

When I'm a - way from you, I'm hap - pi - er than
day or two to think of some - thing

ev - er. Wish I could ex - plain it bet -
clev - er, to write my - self a let -

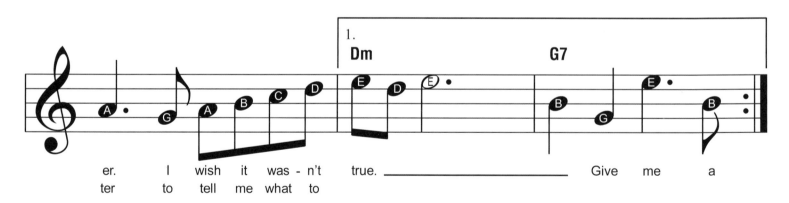

er. I wish it was - n't true. _____ Give me a
ter to tell me what to

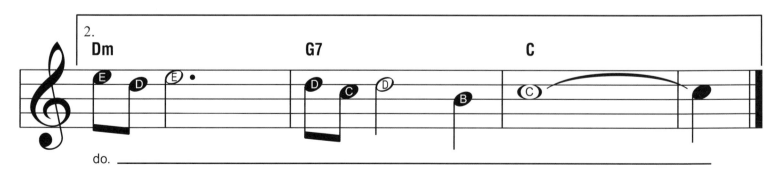

do. _____

Memories

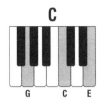
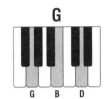

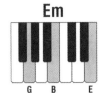
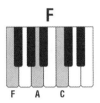

Words and Music by Adam Levine, Jonathan Bellion,
Jordan Johnson, Jacob Hindlin, Stefan Johnson,
Michael Pollack and Vincent Ford

Relaxed half-time groove

Hold On

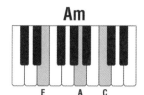
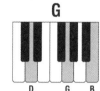

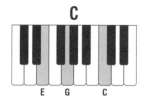

Words and Music by Justin Bieber,
Jon Bellion, Andrew Watt,
Walter De Backer, Ali Tamposi,
Luiz Bonfa and Louis Bell

Moderately fast

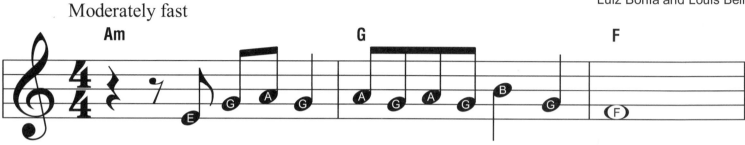

You know you can call me if you need some - one.

(Instrumental)   I'll pick up the piec - es if you come un -

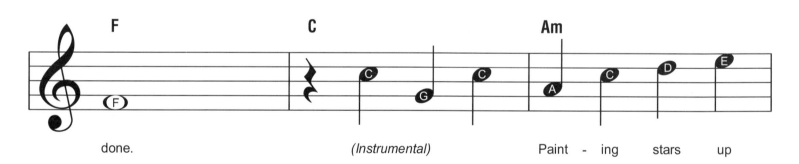

done.   (Instrumental)   Paint - ing stars up

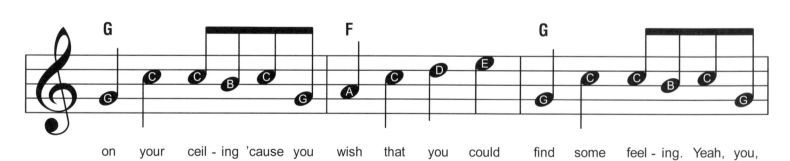

on your ceil - ing 'cause you wish that you could find some feel - ing. Yeah, you,

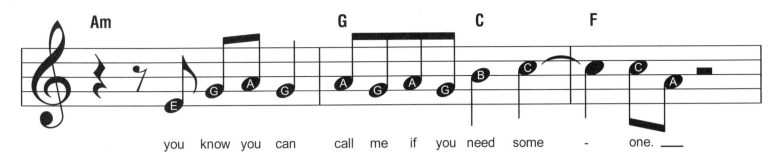

you know you can call me if you need some - one. ___

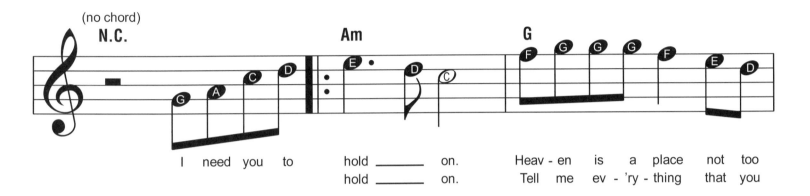

I need you to hold ___ on. Heav - en is a place not too
hold ___ on. Tell me ev - 'ry - thing that you

far a - way. ___ We all know I should be the one to
need to say. ___ 'Cause I know how it feels to be some-

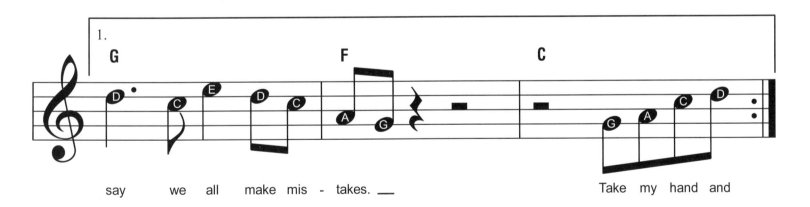

1.
say we all make mis - takes. ___ Take my hand and

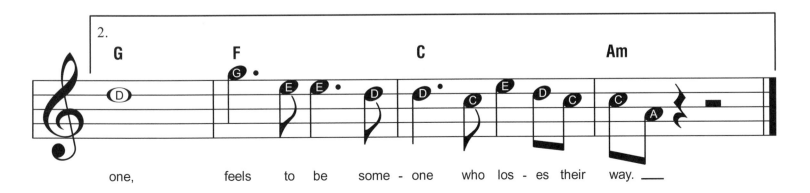

2.
one, feels to be some - one who los - es their way. ___

Kings & Queens

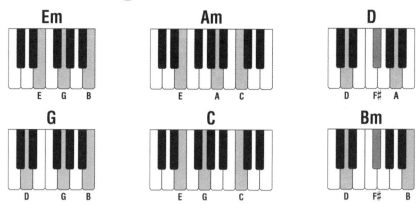

Words and Music by Desmond Child, Amanda Koci,
Brett McLaughlin, Henry Walter, Madison Love,
Mimoza Blinsson, Jakob Erixson,
Nadir Khayat and Hillary Bernstein

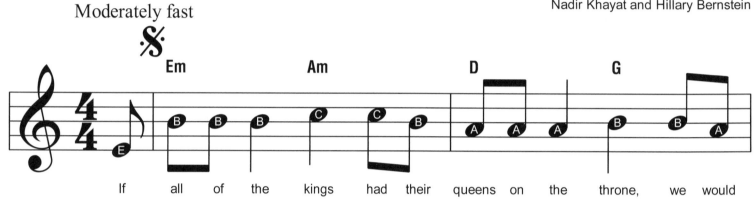

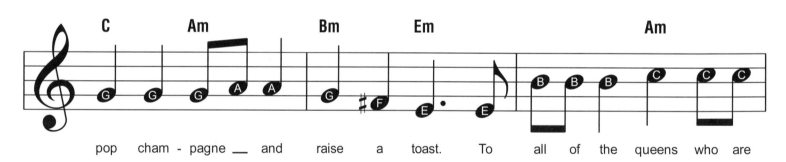

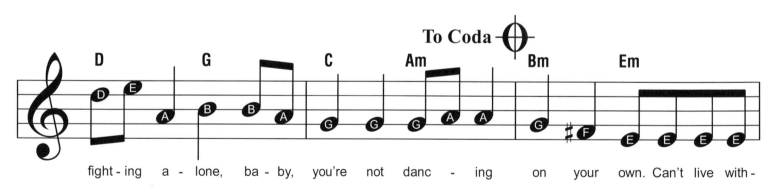

Lose You to Love Me

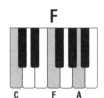

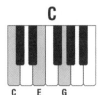

Words and Music by Selena Gomez,
Justin Tranter, Julia Michaels,
Robin Fredriksson and Mattias Larsson

You prom-ised the world and I fell for it.
I saw the signs and I ig-nored it.

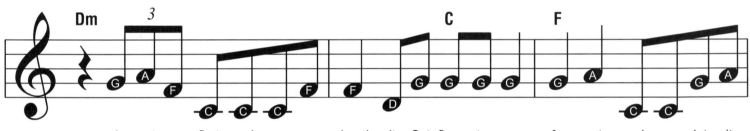

I put you first and you a-dored it. Set fires to my for-est and you let it
Rose-col-ored glass-es all dis-tort-ed. Set fire to my pur-pose and I let it

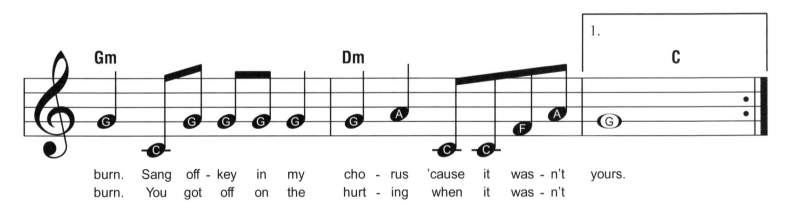

burn. Sang off-key in my cho-rus 'cause it was-n't yours.
burn. You got off on the hurt-ing when it was-n't

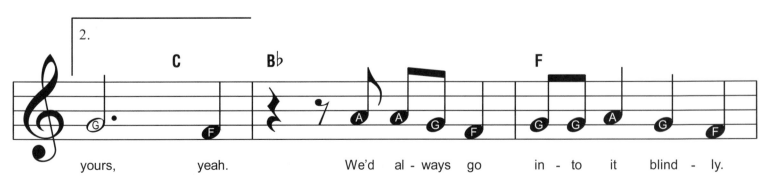

yours, yeah. We'd al-ways go in-to it blind-ly.

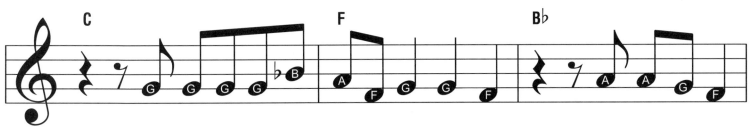

I need-ed to lose ____ you to find me. This dance, it was

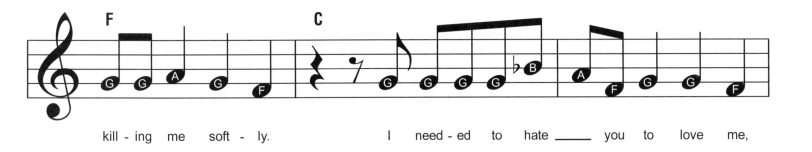

kill-ing me soft-ly. I need-ed to hate ____ you to love me,

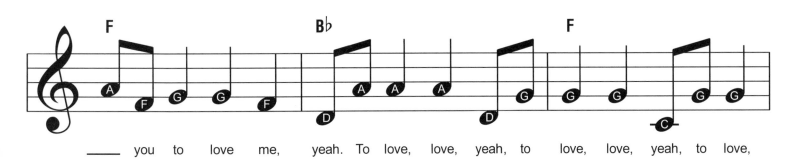

yeah. To love, love, yeah, to love, love, yeah, to love, yeah. I need-ed to lose

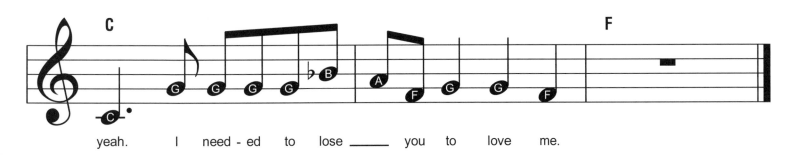

____ you to love me, yeah. To love, love, yeah, to love, love, yeah, to love,

yeah. I need-ed to lose ____ you to love me.

Lover

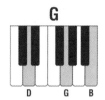
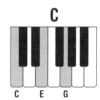
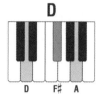

Words and Music by
Taylor Swift

Moderately fast

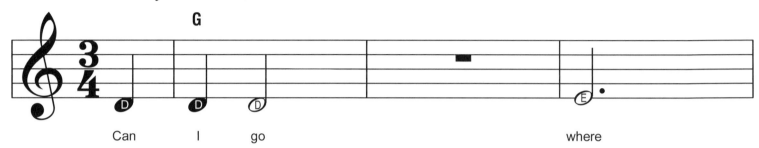

Can I go where

you go? _____ (Instrumental)

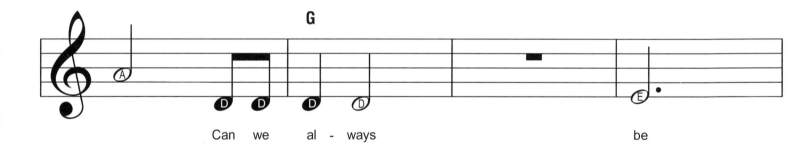

Can we al - ways be

this close? _____ For - ev - er and

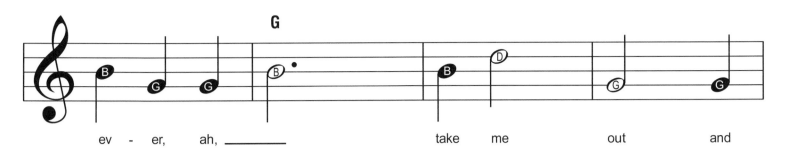

ev - er, ah, _____ take me out and

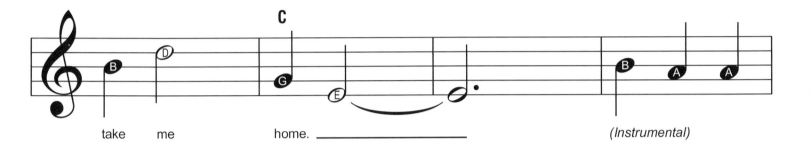

take me home. _____ *(Instrumental)*

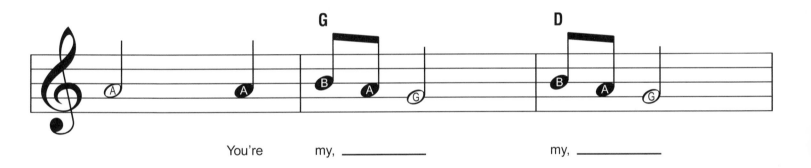

You're my, _____ my, _____

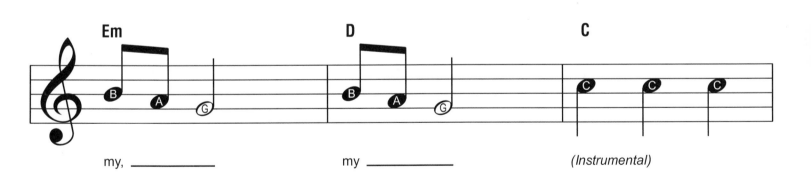

my, _____ my _____ *(Instrumental)*

(no chord)
N.C.

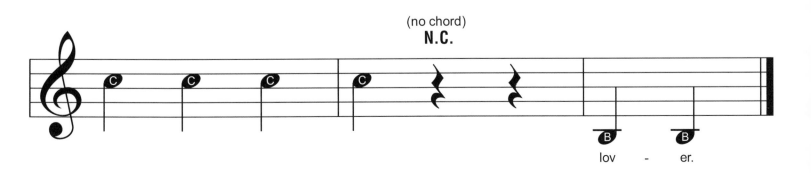

lov - er.

Save Your Tears

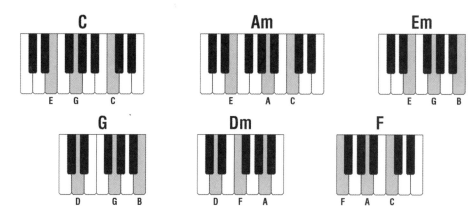

Words and Music by Abel Tesfaye,
Max Martin, Jason Quenneville,
Oscar Holter and Ahmad Balshe

I saw you danc-ing in a crowd-ed room.

You look so hap-py when I'm not with you. But then you

saw me, caught you by sur-prise, a sin-gle tear-drop fall-ing from your eye.

I don't know why I run a-way.

Señorita

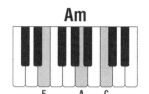
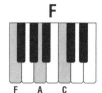
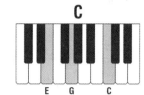
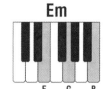
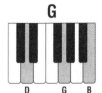

Words and Music by Camila Cabello, Charlotte Aitchison,
Jack Patterson, Shawn Mendes, Magnus Hoiberg,
Benjamin Levin, Ali Tamposi and Andrew Wotman

Moderate Latin groove

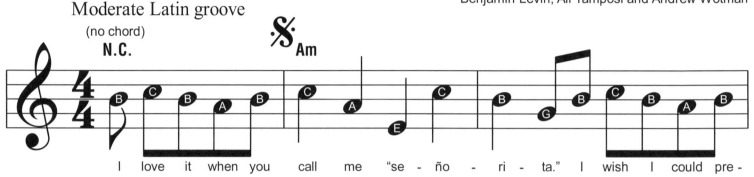

I love it when you call me "se - ño - ri - ta." I wish I could pre -

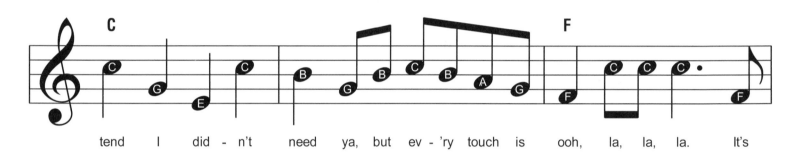

tend I did - n't need ya, but ev - 'ry touch is ooh, la, la, la. It's

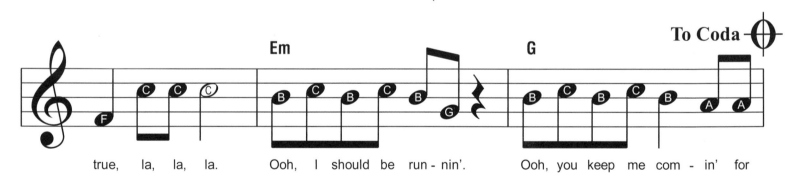

true, la, la, la. Ooh, I should be run - nin'. Ooh, you keep me com - in' for

ya. Land in Mi - am - i, the air was hot from sum - mer

Sunday Best

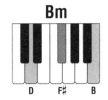
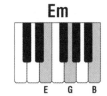
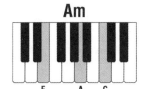
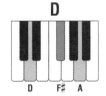

Words and Music by Forrest Frank
and Colin Padalecki

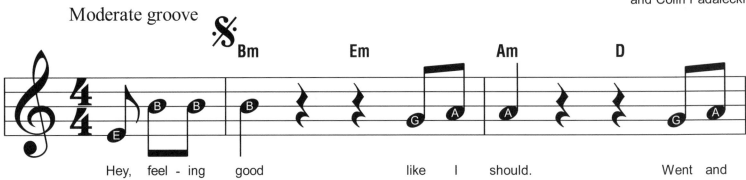

Hey, feel - ing good like I should. Went and

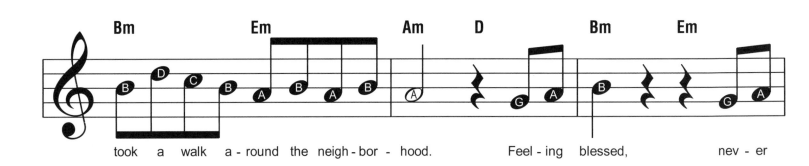

took a walk a - round the neigh - bor - hood. Feel - ing blessed, nev - er

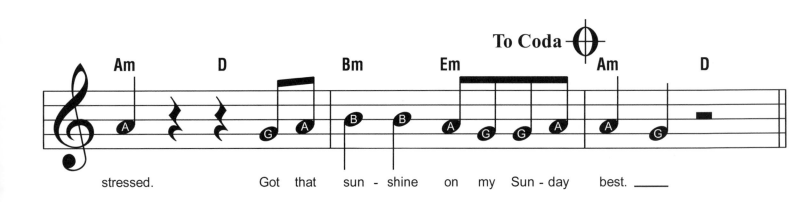

stressed. Got that sun - shine on my Sun - day best. _____

Ev - 'ry day can be a bet - ter day de - spite the chal - lenge.
It's gon - na get dif - fi - cult to stand, but hold your bal - ance.

All you got - ta do is leave it bet - ter than you found it.
I just say "what - ev - er" 'cause there is no way a - round it.

Ev - 'ry - one falls down some - times, but

you just got - ta know it - 'll all be ____ fine. It's o - kay.

Uh - huh. _____ It's o - kay. ____ It's o-

D.S. al Coda
(no chord) (Return to 𝄋, play to 𝄌
and skip to Coda)

CODA

kay. _____ Hey, feel - ing   best. _____

Underdog

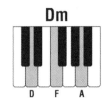
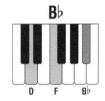
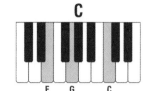
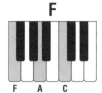

Words and Music by Alicia Augello-Cook,
Ed Sheeran, Amy Wadge,
Foy Vance, Jonny Coffer
and Johnny McDaid

Moderate Shuffle

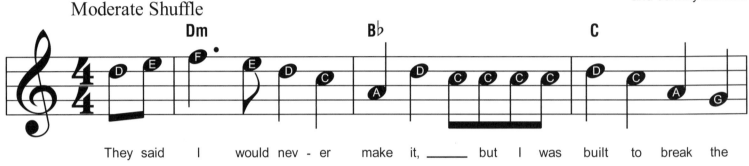

They said I would nev-er make it, _____ but I was built to break the

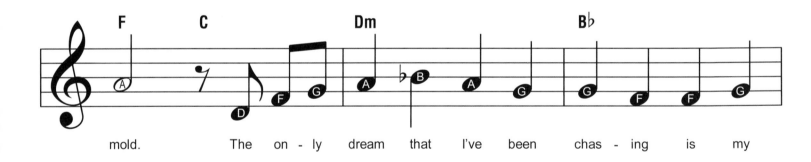

mold. The on-ly dream that I've been chas-ing is my

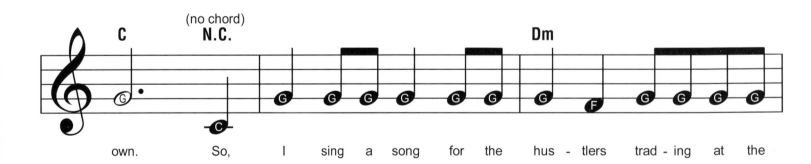

own. So, I sing a song for the hus-tlers trad-ing at the

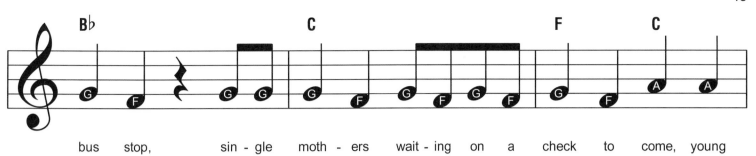

bus stop, sin - gle moth - ers wait - ing on a check to come, young

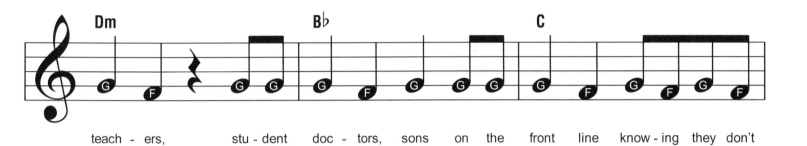

teach - ers, stu - dent doc - tors, sons on the front line know - ing they don't

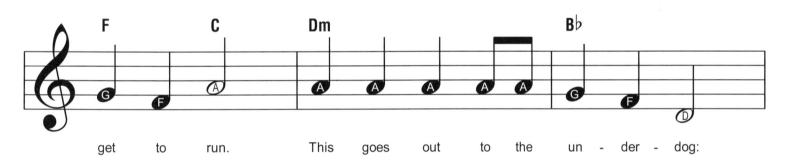

get to run. This goes out to the un - der - dog:

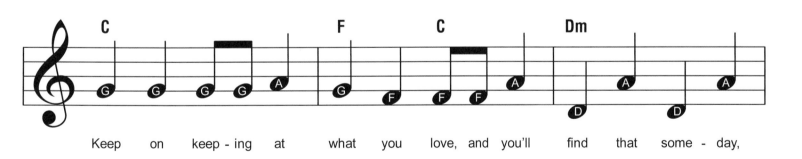

Keep on keep - ing at what you love, and you'll find that some - day,

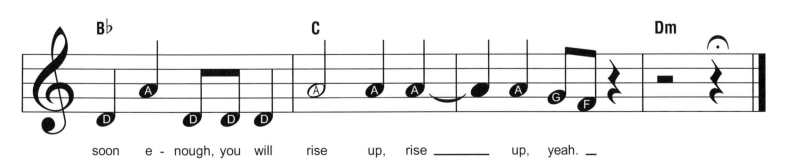

soon e - nough, you will rise up, rise _____ up, yeah. _

Willow

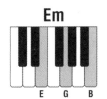

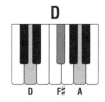
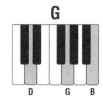
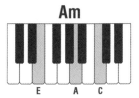

Words and Music by Taylor Swift
and Aaron Dessner

Moderate half-time feel

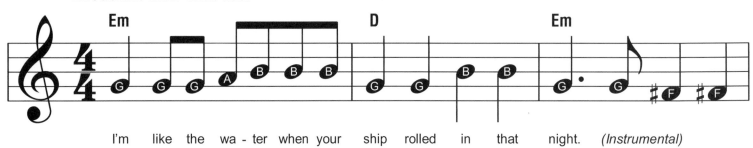

I'm like the wa-ter when your ship rolled in that night. *(Instrumental)*

Rough on the sur-face, but you cut through like a

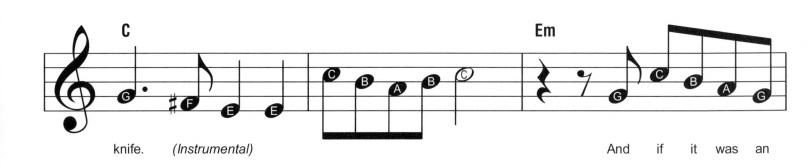

knife. *(Instrumental)* And if it was an

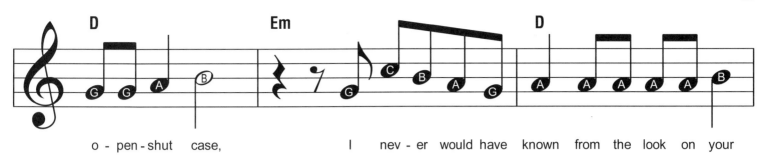

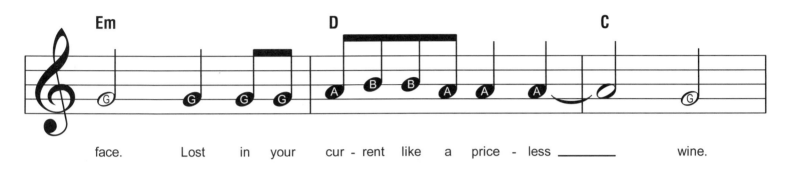

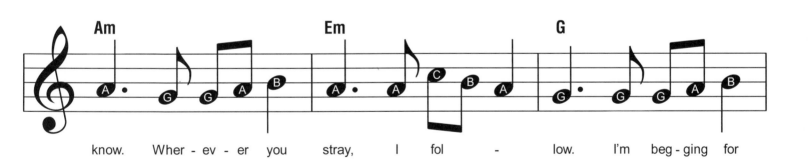

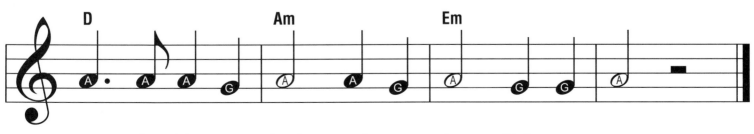

Stay

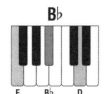
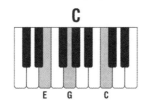

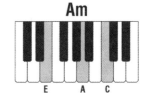

Words and Music by Justin Bieber, Blake Shatkin,
Omer Fedi, Charlie Puth, Charlton Howard,
Michael Mule, Issac DeBoni and Subhaan Rahman

Moderately fast

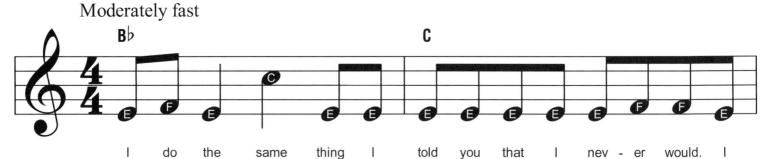

I do the same thing I told you that I nev-er would. I

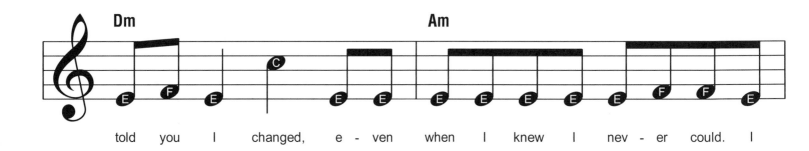

told you I changed, e-ven when I knew I nev-er could. I

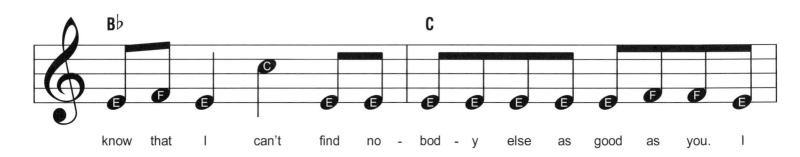

know that I can't find no-bod-y else as good as you. I

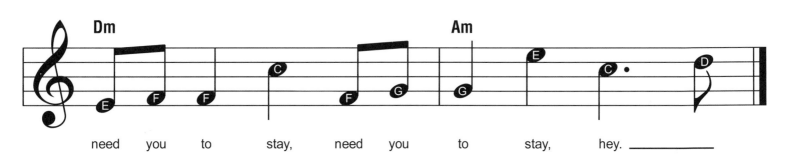

need you to stay, need you to stay, hey. _____

SUPER EASY SONGBOOK

It's super easy! This series features accessible arrangements for piano, with simple right-hand melody, letter names inside each note, and basic left-hand chord diagrams. Perfect for players of all ages!

ADELE
00394705 22 songs.....................................$14.99

THE BEATLES
00198161 60 songs.....................................$15.99

BEAUTIFUL BALLADS
00385162 50 songs.....................................$14.99

BEETHOVEN
00345533 21 selections.............................$9.99

BEST SONGS EVER
00329877 60 songs.....................................$16.99

BROADWAY
00193871 60 songs.....................................$15.99

JOHNNY CASH
00287524 20 songs.......................................$9.99

CHART HITS
00380277 24 songs.....................................$12.99

CHRISTMAS CAROLS
00277955 60 songs.....................................$15.99

CHRISTMAS SONGS
00236850 60 songs.....................................$15.99

CHRISTMAS SONGS WITH 3 CHORDS
00367423 30 songs.....................................$10.99

CLASSIC ROCK
00287526 60 songs.....................................$15.99

CLASSICAL
00194693 60 selections.............................$15.99

COUNTRY
00285257 60 songs.....................................$15.99

DISNEY
00199558 60 songs.....................................$15.99

BOB DYLAN
00364487 22 songs.....................................$12.99

BILLIE EILISH
00346515 22 songs.....................................$10.99

FOLKSONGS
00381031 60 songs.....................................$15.99

FOUR CHORD SONGS
00249533 60 songs.....................................$15.99

FROZEN COLLECTION
00334069 14 songs.....................................$12.99

GEORGE GERSHWIN
00345536 22 songs.......................................$9.99

GOSPEL
00285256 60 songs.....................................$15.99

HIT SONGS
00194367 60 songs.....................................$16.99

HYMNS
00194659 60 songs.....................................$15.99

JAZZ STANDARDS
00233687 60 songs.....................................$15.99

BILLY JOEL
00329996 22 songs.....................................$11.99

ELTON JOHN
00298762 22 songs.....................................$10.99

KIDS' SONGS
00198009 60 songs.....................................$16.99

LEAN ON ME
00350593 22 songs.....................................$10.99

THE LION KING
00303511 9 songs...$9.99

ANDREW LLOYD WEBBER
00249580 48 songs.....................................$19.99

MOVIE SONGS
00233670 60 songs.....................................$15.99

PEACEFUL MELODIES
00367880 60 songs.....................................$16.99

POP SONGS FOR KIDS
00346809 60 songs.....................................$16.99

POP STANDARDS
00233770 60 songs.....................................$16.99

QUEEN
00294889 20 songs.....................................$10.99

ED SHEERAN
00287525 20 songs.......................................$9.99

SIMPLE SONGS
00329906 60 songs.....................................$15.99

STAR WARS (EPISODES I–IX)
00345560 17 songs.....................................$12.99

HARRY STYLES
01069721 15 songs.....................................$12.99

TAYLOR SWIFT
1192568 30 songs.......................................$14.99

THREE CHORD SONGS
00249664 60 songs.....................................$16.99

TOP HITS
00300405 22 songs.....................................$10.99

WORSHIP
00294871 60 songs.....................................$16.99

HAL•LEONARD

Disney characters and artwork TM & © 2021 Disney

Prices, contents and availability subject to change without notice.

www.halleonard.com

0723
327

INSTANT Piano Songs

Audio Access Included

The **Instant Piano Songs** series will help you play your favorite songs quickly and easily — whether you use one hand or two! Start with the melody in your right hand, adding basic left-hand chords when you're ready. Letter names inside each note speed up the learning process, and optional rhythm patterns take your playing to the next level. Online backing tracks are also included. Stream or download the tracks using the unique code inside each book, then play along to build confidence and sound great!

THE BEATLES

All My Loving · Blackbird · Can't Buy Me Love · Eleanor Rigby · Get Back · Here, There and Everywhere · Hey Jude · I Will · Let It Be · Michelle · Nowhere Man · Ob-La-Di, Ob-La-Da · Penny Lane · When I'm Sixty-Four · With a Little Help from My Friends · Yesterday · and more.
00295926 Book/Online Audio $14.99

BROADWAY'S BEST

All I Ask of You · Bring Him Home · Defying Gravity · Don't Cry for Me Argentina · Edelweiss · Memory · The Music of the Night · On My Own · People · Seasons of Love · Send in the Clowns · She Used to Be Mine · Sunrise, Sunset · Tonight · Waving Through a Window · and more.
00323342 Book/Online Audio $14.99

CHRISTMAS CLASSICS

Angels We Have Heard on High · Away in a Manger · Deck the Hall · The First Noel · Good King Wenceslas · Hark! the Herald Angels Sing · Jingle Bells · Jolly Old St. Nicholas · Joy to the World · O Christmas Tree · Up on the Housetop · We Three Kings of Orient Are · We Wish You a Merry Christmas · What Child Is This? · and more.
00348326 Book/Online Audio $14.99

CHRISTMAS STANDARDS

All I Want for Christmas Is You · Christmas Time Is Here · Frosty the Snow Man · Grown-Up Christmas List · A Holly Jolly Christmas · I'll Be Home for Christmas · Jingle Bell Rock · The Little Drummer Boy · Mary, Did You Know? · Merry Christmas, Darling · Rudolph the Red-Nosed Reindeer · White Christmas · and more.
00294854 Book/Online Audio $14.99

CLASSICAL THEMES

Canon (Pachelbel) · Für Elise (Beethoven) · Jesu, Joy of Man's Desiring (Bach) · Jupiter (Holst) · Lullaby (Brahms) · Pomp and Circumstance (Elgar) · Spring (Vivaldi) · Symphony No. 9, Fourth Movement ("Ode to Joy") (Beethoven) · and more.
00283826 Book/Online Audio $14.99

DISNEY FAVORITES

Beauty and the Beast · Can You Feel the Love Tonight · Chim Chim Cher-ee · Colors of the Wind · A Dream Is a Wish Your Heart Makes · Friend Like Me · How Far I'll Go · It's a Small World · Kiss the Girl · Lava · Let It Go · Mickey Mouse March · Part of Your World · Reflection · Remember Me (Ernesto de la Cruz) · A Whole New World · You'll Be in My Heart (Pop Version) · and more.
00283720 Book/Online Audio $14.99

HITS OF 2010-2019

All About That Bass (Meghan Trainor) · All of Me (John Legend) · Can't Stop the Feeling (Justin Timberlake) · Happy (Pharrell Williams) · Hey, Soul Sister (Train) · Just the Way You Are (Bruno Mars) · Rolling in the Deep (Adele) · Shallow (Lady Gaga & Bradley Cooper) · Shake It Off (Taylor Swift) · Shape of You (Ed Sheeran) · and more.
00345364 Book/Online Audio $14.99

KIDS' POP SONGS

Adore You (Harry Styles) · Cool Kids (AJR) · Drivers License (Olivia Rodrigo) · How Far I'll Go (from Moana) · A Million Dreams (from The Greatest Showman) · Ocean Eyes (Billie Eilish) · Shake It Off (Taylor Swift) · What Makes You Beautiful (One Direction) · and more.
00371694 Book/Online Audio $14.99

MOVIE SONGS

As Time Goes By · City of Stars · Endless Love · Hallelujah · I Will Always Love You · Laura · Moon River · My Heart Will Go on (Love Theme from 'Titanic') · Over the Rainbow · Singin' in the Rain · Skyfall · Somewhere Out There · Stayin' Alive · Tears in Heaven · Unchained Melody · Up Where We Belong · The Way We Were · What a Wonderful World · and more.
00283718 Book/Online Audio $14.99

POP HITS

All of Me · Chasing Cars · Despacito · Feel It Still · Havana · Hey, Soul Sister · Ho Hey · I'm Yours · Just Give Me a Reason · Love Yourself · Million Reasons · Perfect · Riptide · Shake It Off · Stay with Me · Thinking Out Loud · Viva La Vida · What Makes You Beautiful · and more.
00283825 Book/Online Audio $15.99

SONGS FOR KIDS

Do-Re-Mi · Hakuna Matata · It's a Small World · On Top of Spaghetti · Puff the Magic Dragon · The Rainbow Connection · SpongeBob SquarePants Theme Song · Take Me Out to the Ball Game · Tomorrow · The Wheels on the Bus · Won't You Be My Neighbor? (It's a Beautiful Day in the Neighborhood) · You Are My Sunshine · and more.
00323352 Book/Online Audio $15.99

HAL·LEONARD®
www.halleonard.com